Hugh Grant

Hugh Grant Biography

Charming the world: From Rom-Com Royalty to Cultural Icon

Stephen P. Cox

Hugh Grant

All rights reserved. No part of this publication may be reproduced, distributed or transmitted in any form or by any means, including photocopying, recording, or other electronic or mechanical methods, without the prior written permission of the publisher, except in the case of brief quotations embodied in critical reviews and certain other noncommercial uses permitted by this law

Copyright© Stephen P. Cox, 2024.

Hugh Grant

Table of contents

Overview

Hugh Grant's Career Highlights in Brief

Chapter 1: Background and Early Life
- Family Dynamics and Siblings
- Hugo Grant's Childhood and Education
- Hugh Grant's Early Interests and Influences

Chapter 2: Becoming an Actor
- Initiation into Acting
- The Pioneering Contributions of Hugh Grant
- The Early Difficulties and Triumphs of Hugh Grant

Chapter 3: Ascent to Notoriety
- Notoriety and Financial Success
- Notable Hugh Grant Performances and Film
- Notable Partnerships with Co-Stars and Directors
- Recognitions and Submissions

Hugh Grant

Chapter 4: Characterizing Hugh Grant in Classic Movies
- Public perception and media attention
- Individual Difficulties
- Career Accomplishments

Chapter 5: Career Development
- First Moves in the Direction of Dramatic Roles
- Industry Recognition and Critical Acclaim
- Notable Later Motion Pictures and TV Series
- Input toward Film Production
- Fostering Innovative Projects and Up-and-Coming Talent

Chapter 6: Honors and Commendations
- Acclaim from the Industry and Critics
- Early Career and Stardom in Romantic Comedies
- Recognition in the Industry

Chapter 7: Activism and Philanthropy

Hugh Grant

- Charitable Activities and Issues Hugh Grant Endorses
- Activism in Politics and Society

Chapter 8: Legacy and Effects
- Reimagining the Romantic Comedy
- Increasing to Dramatic Positions
- Input to the British Film Industry
- Popularity and Cultural Impact
- Views from Critics and Peers
- Major Ideas in Thoughts
- Enduring Inputs into Film

summary

Hugh Grant

Overview

For more than thirty years, Hugh Grant has played a pivotal role in British film and is a highly regarded performer across the globe. Acclaimed for his distinctly endearing and frequently self-deprecating roles in romantic comedies, Grant has distinguished himself in the motion picture industry.

1. Cultural Icon of Romantic Comedy: Due to his roles in movies such as "Love Actually," "Notting Hill," and "Four Weddings and a Funeral," Grant has become widely recognized in the romantic comedy genre. His ability to combine charisma, sensitivity, and humor has made him a beloved character to audiences worldwide and established a new bar for leading men in romance movies.

2. Actor Versatility: Although Grant is best known for his romantic comedy parts, his work spans a wide spectrum. In movies like "Florence Foster Jenkins" and "Paddington 2," he has adeptly embraced more dramatic

and varied parts, showcasing his versatility and nuance as an actor. He has avoided being stereotyped and received critical recognition thanks to his adaptability.

3. Longevity and Consistency: Grant's consistent success throughout the years demonstrates his talent and enduring appeal. He has been able to stay current and in demand, taking on important jobs late into his career, in contrast to many performers who gain recognition and then fade away.

4. Impact on British movies: Grant has been instrumental in bringing British films to a global audience. His movies are frequently among the best-selling British exports, and his persona has elevated the UK film industry's profile internationally. This international appeal has helped British cinema maintain its strong position and solid reputation as a producer of high-caliber pictures.

5. Activism & Philanthropy: Hugh Grant is well-known for his activism and philanthropic endeavors in addition

to his filmography. He has supported topics like press control and privacy rights by using his platform and involvement in several humanitarian endeavors. Outside the entertainment world, he is respected for his candidness and willingness to speak out on significant problems.

6. Success on Both the Critical and Commercial Fronts: Grant's career is distinguished by a combination of both types of success. His films have frequently been box office successes, and he has won multiple accolades and been nominated for several more, including BAFTAs and Golden Globes. His enormous influence on the cinema business is further demonstrated by his combination of critical and commercial success.

7. Durable Popularity: Grant's enduring appeal is a reflection of both his skill and the love that people feel for him. He has become one of the most adored performers of his generation because of his ability to engage audiences, whether it is in a funny or emotional romantic scene.

Hugh Grant

Hugh Grant is significant and influential because of his acting range, his ability to captivate audiences, his contributions to British cinema, and his involvement in social causes and philanthropy. His reputation in the film industry is one of talent, charm, and enduring impact.

Hugh Grant's Career Highlights in Brief

1. Early Professional Life and Breakthrough: "Maurice" (1987): Grant's portrayal as Clive Durham in this adaptation of E.M. Forster's book, which served as his big screen debut.

2. "Four Weddings and a Funeral" (1994): This movie was a sea change for Grant, catapulting him to global recognition. His performance as the endearing, fumbling Charles won him the Best Actor Golden Globe.

3. Romantic Comedy Stardom: "Notting Hill" (1999): Grant played a modest bookshop owner opposite Julia

Hugh Grant

Roberts in this well-loved romantic comedy, cementing his place as the genre's leading man.

4. Grant's portrayal of the roguish Daniel Cleaver in "Bridget Jones's Diary" (2001) and "Bridget Jones: The Edge of Reason" (2004) was a fan favorite, demonstrating his comedic timing and charisma on screen.

5. Grant's performance of the British Prime Minister in the ensemble romantic comedy "Love Actually" (2003) expanded his repertoire of memorable roles.

6. Diversifying Roles: "About a Boy" (2002): Grant demonstrated his ability to strike a balance between humor and more in-depth, nuanced character work in his portrayal of the naive, self-centered Will Freeman.

7. "Florence Foster Jenkins" (2016): Grant received positive reviews from critics and multiple nominations for awards, including a BAFTA, for his performance as the title character's devoted husband, St. Clair Bayfield.

8. Lately, Grant has received widespread appreciation for his portrayal of the colorful villain Phoenix Buchanan in "Paddington 2" (2017), which also earned him a nomination for a BAFTA.

9. In the BBC miniseries "A Very English Scandal" (2018), Grant played politician Jeremy Thorpe. The role earned him praise from critics and multiple nominations for awards.

10. Sustained Success and Legacy: Hugh Grant has consistently combined critically praised roles with box office successes over his career. He has remained current in the industry thanks to his capacity to reinvent himself and take on a variety of jobs.

His contributions to the movie industry, especially in the romantic comedy genre, have had a profound effect and he is still a well-liked character.

Highlights of Hugh Grant's career, like his breakout role in "Four Weddings and a Funeral" and his critically

Hugh Grant

lauded roles in "Paddington 2" and "A Very English Scandal," demonstrate his adaptability and timeless appeal.

Chapter 1: Background and Early Life

On September 9, 1960, Hugh John Mungo Grant was born in Hammersmith, London, England. His parents are James Murray Grant and Fynvola Susan MacLean. His upbringing in a household with a wide range of ancestry and a strong academic foundation prepared him for his success in the entertainment business.

Hugh Grant's diverse identity is influenced by his family's mixture of Scottish, English, Welsh, and Irish ancestry. His father's grandpa, Major James Murray Grant, was highly commended for valor and tenacity during World War II, highlighting a strong and courageous family history. Hugh's maternal side boasts illustrious ancestors, his mother's scholastic endeavors bolstered by her grandfather's military experience.

James Murray Grant, the son of James and Fynvola Grant, began his professional life as a salesman with a focus on carpets before turning to the arts. His later ventures showed a flexible approach to work, including starting his own rug company. James's son was also exposed to discipline and perseverance from his time serving in the British Army with the Seaforth Highlanders.

Fynvola Grant, née MacLean, was a renowned teacher renowned for her commitment to academic excellence and scholarly insight. Her teaching career included Latin, French, and music at schools like West London's St. Paul's Girls' School, where she fostered her students' intellectual development. Hugh was greatly impacted by Fynvola's love of reading and the arts as a child, which helped him develop a passion for acting and storytelling.

Family Dynamics and Siblings

James Grant, Hugh Grant's elder brother, led a largely reclusive life away from the public eye during their childhood. The Grant brothers' close-knit upbringing, influenced by parental guidance and academic stimulation, was reflected in their bond of family values and mutual support.

The Grant family in Hammersmith offered a supportive atmosphere enhanced by thoughtful conversation and an appreciation of art. Hugh's early development was aided by books, conversations about current events, and cultural events, which sparked his interest in performing arts and literature.

Hugh Grant's upbringing in a household with a wide range of ancestry and a dedication to learning and the arts set the stage for his success as an actor in the future. The virtues of perseverance, intellectual curiosity, and artistic expression that continue to define his personal and professional activities were reinforced by the supportive influence of his parents, James Murray Grant and Fynvola Susan MacLean, as well as the familial bond he shared with his brother, James.

Hugh Grant

Hugo Grant's Childhood and Education

Born in Hammersmith, London, England, on September 9, 1960, Hugh John Mungo Grant became one of Hollywood's most famous faces, known for his charm, wit, and versatility on screen. His rise from a boyhood in London to international renown was characterized by a combination of creative influence, academic rigor, and a growing love for performance arts.

The second child of James Murray Grant and Fynvola Susan MacLean was Hugh Grant. James, his father, was a carpet salesman for a while before deciding to become an artist. James also had military experience, having been an officer in the British Army's Seaforth Highlanders. Fynvola, his mother, was a renowned educator who taught Latin, French, and music and was highly intelligent. She was a teacher at several institutions, including the prestigious West London St. Paul's Girls' School.

Hugh Grant

Hugh was raised in an intellectually stimulating environment at the Grant home, where books and conversations about literature and the arts were commonplace. Hugh and his older brother James Grant were greatly influenced by Fynvola's love of learning and her commitment to fostering her kids' intellectual curiosity. James Grant chose to stay out of the spotlight throughout Hugh's climb to stardom.

Hugh Grant started his school career at Hogarth Primary School in the West London neighborhood of Chiswick. He later pursued his education at Hammersmith's St Peter's Primary School, where he first showed signs of academic promise and a natural aptitude for the theatrical arts. His enrollment in Latymer Upper School, an independent school renowned for its academic brilliance and heavy emphasis on the arts and humanities, was a turning point in his transfer to secondary education.

Grant's love of theater and literature blossomed in Latymer Upper. He took an active part in school plays, which helped him hone his acting abilities and cultivate a strong love of narrative. His professional objectives were greatly influenced by his teachers, who saw his talent and encouraged him to explore several aspects of the performing arts.

Grant was exposed to the performing arts in contexts other than school plays. He got plenty of chances to see plays, concerts, and movie screenings while growing up in London, a city known for its theaters and creative energy. His desire to be in the entertainment sector was cemented and his love of acting was further stoked by these encounters.

During Grant's early years, the theater and classic literature he encountered had a profound effect on his artistic sensibility. He gained a deep comprehension of character development, plot structure, and storytelling nuances—a fundamental skill that would eventually set his on-screen performances apart.

Hugh Grant

After graduating from Latymer Upper High School, Hugh Grant had to make a crucial choice about his future academic and professional trajectory. He attended the esteemed New College, Oxford, to further his studies after receiving encouragement from his professors and being motivated by his early exposure to the performing arts. Grant studied English literature at Oxford and fully engaged in the intellectual and cultural life of the university.

His experience at Oxford further deepened his understanding of storytelling and narrative dynamics by giving him priceless insights into literature and critical thinking. Grant also had lots of opportunities to hone his acting abilities by taking part in student performances and theatrical workshops thanks to the university's well-known theater scene.

Hugh Grant's growing interest in acting developed further while he was a student at Oxford. He was an active member of the Oxford University Dramatic Society (OUDS), a prestigious organization that has a

Hugh Grant

long history of supporting up-and-coming performers. He was able to work with other aspiring actors and directors through OUDS, which helped him hone his craft and get ready for the challenges he would face in the workplace.

Grant's remarkable career in the entertainment sector began when he made the switch from college to professional acting. He started on a path marked by tenacity and resolve, overcoming obstacles along the way and grasping chances to display his skill on stage and screen.

Hugh Grant's early years and schooling prepared him for his extraordinary acting career, which was marked by a combination of rigorous academic study, creative influence, and a deep love of narrative. Grant's journey, which began with his early years in London and continued with his academic endeavors at Oxford University, is indicative of his dedication to perfection and his abiding passion for the performing arts.

Hugh Grant

With his captivating performances, Grant has captured viewers' attention throughout his career, proving his flexibility in a variety of genres and solidifying his status as a key character in modern film. His lasting appeal and cultural influence bear witness to the early life lessons and educational chances that molded his creative character and catapulted him to international recognition.

Hugh Grant's Early Interests and Influences

Hugh Grant showed early signs of a natural affinity for the arts, which he attributed to his upbringing in London's culturally rich surroundings and his parents' encouraging influence.

1. Parental Influence: Hugh Grant's early interests were greatly influenced by his parents, James Murray Grant and Fynvola Susan MacLean. His mother fostered in him a love of reading and storytelling. She was a committed teacher who had a passion for languages and literature. Hugh was introduced to a wide variety of stories and

characters by Fynvola, who was well-versed in ancient literature. This helped to develop Hugh's imagination and form his early reading choices.

2. Early Reading Habits: Books provided Grant with an escape into worlds full of humor, adventure, and profound insights, making them an essential part of his early years. His extensive reading habits included a wide spectrum of literary genres, from modern to classic novels, which helped him to develop an understanding of complex narrative and character development.

3. Theatrical Exposure: London's Cultural Landscape: Hugh Grant had unrivaled access to live performances and artistic experiences as a child growing up in this multicultural city known for its theatrical legacy. He was exposed to a wide range of productions, from avant-garde performances to Shakespearean plays, by the city's thriving theater culture, which sparked his interest in the transformational potential of stagecraft.

Hugh Grant

4. Early Theater Engagements: Grant had the chance to explore his developing interest in acting through his participation in school plays and neighborhood theater shows. These early encounters gave him the chance to try out several parts, hone his stage presence, and polish his acting abilities under the watchful eye of encouraging role models and drama teachers.

5. Hugh Grant's early interests in theater and literature came together in his quest for artistic development and creative expression. His preferred method of expressing feelings, ideas, and social criticism was narrative; this was a recurring motif in both his acting and filmmaking careers.

6. Cultural Influences: In addition to his academic schooling and theater experiences, Grant's artistic growth was influenced by a wider range of cultural mediums, such as music, visual arts, and film. He welcomed the variety of artistic expressions and let a wide range of sources inspire his developing aesthetic sensibilities.

Hugh Grant

Hugh Grant's early passions and influences combined a strong appreciation for theatrical performance with a love of literature, laying the groundwork for his eventual success in the entertainment sector. Under the guidance of his parents and enhanced by the cultural environment of London, Grant's early years fostered a creative spirit that would come to define his artistic journey. The enduring influence of his early influences on his multifaceted career is evident in his acclaimed body of work, which reflects his dedication to storytelling and exploration of diverse narratives.

Chapter 2: Becoming an Actor

Hugh Grant first got involved in acting while attending Latymer Upper School in Hammersmith, London, where he took part in several school productions. This foundational experience continued at New College, Oxford, where Grant studied English literature and became actively involved in the Oxford University Dramatic Society (OUDS). His comedic timing and ability to embody complex characters shone through early roles, such as Sir Andrew Aguecheek in "Twelfth Night." His roles in OUDS productions, such as "Hamlet," cemented his love of acting and introduced him to mentors and powerful peers.

In 1982, Grant made his feature film debut in "Privileged," a student-produced movie supported by the Oxford Film Foundation. Despite its lackluster results, it gave valuable exposure. He then had small parts in

Hugh Grant

British TV shows like "Jenny's War" and "The Last Place on Earth."

With "Maurice" (1987), Grant's breakthrough came from the adaptation of E.M. Forster's book, in which his performance as Clive Durham won the Venice Film Festival Silver Lion and received critical praise. With this performance, Grant became recognized as a gifted young actor and laid the groundwork for his subsequent achievements and illustrious film career.

Initiation into Acting

Hugh Grant's introduction to acting was a lengthy process marked by early experimentation, scholastic ambitions, and an increasing enthusiasm for performing. His journey from school plays to the professional stage and cinema was defined by tenacity, talent, and a little serendipity.

1. Latymer Upper School: Grant's first taste of acting came during his time at Latymer Upper School in

Hugh Grant

Hammersmith, London. Known for its strong emphasis on arts and humanities, Latymer created an environment suitable for cultivating budding talent. Grant participated in many school performances, discovering his aptitude for acting and polishing his skills in front of an audience.

2. Influential Performances: One of Grant's outstanding early roles was in the school's performance of "Twelfth Night" by William Shakespeare. Playing the role of Sir Andrew Aguecheek, Grant demonstrated his comedic timing and ability to depict complex personalities. These early performances were vital in boosting his confidence and cementing his enthusiasm to pursue acting further.

3. Oxford Education: After finishing his secondary education, Hugh Grant attended New College, Oxford, where he studied English literature. Oxford's rich intellectual and cultural atmosphere afforded him several opportunities to expand his understanding of literature and drama.

4. Involvement in OUDS: While in Oxford, Grant became actively associated with the Oxford University Dramatic Society (OUDS), one of the oldest and most prestigious university drama groups in the UK. His participation in OUDS allowed him to engage with other aspiring actors and directors, appear in a range of plays, and further polish his acting techniques.

Grant's performances in university productions, such as his portrayal of Hamlet in Shakespeare's "Hamlet" and roles in other classical and contemporary plays, drew notice and appreciation from peers and teachers. These experiences not only boosted his acting credentials but also connected him with a network of significant personalities in the world of theater.

5. First Professional Roles: After graduating from Oxford, Hugh Grant had the difficult job of breaking into the professional acting industry. His first professional appearance occurred in 1982 with the film "Privileged," a student-produced film supported by the Oxford Film Foundation. With the starring role, Grant was able to

Hugh Grant

make a name for himself in the industry thanks to the film's modest success.

6. Television and Small Parts: After "Privileged," Grant landed several small parts in movies and television shows. He made appearances in episodes of British television shows, including Jenny's War (1985) and The Last Place on Earth (1985). Even though they weren't well-known parts, these early ones gave him invaluable on-set experience and exposure to the business.

7. "Maurice" (1987): Grant made his feature picture debut in the adaptation of E.M. James Ivory helmed Forster's book. Grant played the young nobleman Clive Durham, who is struggling with his sexuality. His portrayal received high praise from critics. Due to the movie's success at several film festivals, including the Venice Film Festival, where it took home the Silver Lion, Grant became well-known and became recognized as a talented young actor.

Hugh Grant

8. Creating Momentum: After "Maurice," Grant acted in movies such as "The Lair of the White Worm" (1988) and "The Dawning" (1988), which helped him continue to create momentum. Despite the differences in genre and scale between these parts, his acting range and versatility were evident.

Hugh Grant's early acting training provided a solid basis for his subsequent success in the motion picture business. Grant's path into acting was characterized by commitment, skill, and several crucial chances, spanning from school plays and university performances to his first professional appearances. His breakthrough role in "Maurice" laid the groundwork for an illustrious career by demonstrating his capacity to enthrall audiences with subtle performances and a distinct combination of charm and profundity. Hugh Grant's early acting career is a monument to his enduring passion for the craft and his constant devotion to creative excellence, as he went from being a promising rookie to an established actor.

Hugh Grant

The Pioneering Contributions of Hugh Grant

Hugh Grant's ascent to fame was paved with several breakthrough parts that highlighted his charm, actorly ability, and nuance. These parts solidified his status in popular culture and made him a starring man in the film business.

"Maurice" (1987) Clive Durham as the role Synopsis: James Ivory's film "Maurice," an adaptation of E.M. A young guy in early 20th-century England struggles with his sexuality in Forster's book.

Impact: Grant received praise from critics for his portrayal of the conflicted aristocrat Clive Durham. Due to the film's success at the Venice Film Festival, where it took home the Silver Lion, Grant gained a lot of recognition and solidified his reputation as a serious actor who can play roles that are emotionally complicated and nuanced.

Hugh Grant

Role: "Charles"; Synopsis: Directed by Mike Newell, "Four Weddings and a Funeral" (1994) tells the story of Charles and his pals as they negotiate relationships and love throughout a string of social events.

Impact: Both critically and monetarily, the movie was an unexpected hit. Despite having a small budget, it became one of the highest-grossing British films of all time, earning nearly $245 million worldwide. Grant became well-known throughout the world and won a Golden Globe for Best Actor in a Motion Picture Musical or Comedy for his depiction of Charles. His charmingly awkward yet funny performance struck a chord with viewers and made him a main man in romantic comedies.

"Sense and Sensibility" (1995): Role: "Edward Ferrars" Synopsis: Ang Lee's adaptation of Jane Austen's beloved novel centers on the Dashwood sisters and their quest for both love and financial stability.

Hugh Grant

Impact: For his sensitive and nuanced portrayal of the nice but confused suitor Edward Ferrars, Grant received high appreciation. With numerous accolades and nominations for the movie, Grant's standing as a versatile performer who can shine in historical dramas was further cemented.

"Notting Hill" (1999): "William Thacker" Synopsis: "Notting Hill," a romantic comedy helmed by Roger Michell, follows the story of a modest London bookshop owner who develops feelings for a well-known American actress played by Julia Roberts.

Impact: The movie became a revered classic after becoming a tremendous commercial success. Grant cemented his reputation as a leading actor in the romantic comedy genre with his depiction of the charming and self-deprecating William Thacker, which struck a chord with viewers all over the world.

"Bridget Jones's Diary" (2001): Role: "Daniel Cleaver" Synopsis: Directed by Sharon Maguire and based on

Hugh Grant

Helen Fielding's novel, "Bridget Jones's Diary" follows Bridget Jones as she negotiates a love triangle and other personal and professional obstacles.

Impact: Grant demonstrated his ability to play against type in his portrayal as the endearing but roguish Daniel Cleaver. His portrayal gave the movie's love triangle an additional level of nuance, and its box-office success confirmed his adaptability and attractiveness to romantic comedies.

"About a Boy" (2002), directed by Chris and Paul Weitz, is a film version of Nick Hornby's novel about a carefree bachelor who develops an unusual friendship with a little kid. Will Freeman plays the lead role.

Impact: Grant showed off his range as an actor by portraying Will Freeman in a humorous and heartfelt way. Grant's filmography gained depth and received critical acclaim, demonstrating his ability to play roles with more nuance and maturity.

Hugh Grant

The films "Maurice," "Four Weddings and a Funeral," "Sense and Sensibility," "Notting Hill," "Bridget Jones's Diary," and "About a Boy" marked Hugh Grant's breakout roles and made him a highly adored and versatile actor of his generation. These parts solidified his place in the annals of cinema history while also showcasing his talent and charisma.

The Early Difficulties and Triumphs of Hugh Grant

The path to fame for Hugh Grant wasn't without its challenges. Perseverance, hard effort, and a string of crucial opportunities marked the early years of his career and laid the path for his eventual success.

First difficulties

1. Struggles to Find Roles: Following his graduation from Oxford's New College, where he majored in English literature, Grant encountered the usual obstacles faced by budding actors. He had to negotiate the cutthroat world of the performing profession, going on

multiple auditions and frequently being turned down for parts.

2. Typecasting Concerns: Grant ran the risk of being stereotyped at the beginning of his career. Offers for roles resembling his own, despite his naturally endearing and somewhat restrained manner, threatened to curtail his range as an actor.

3. Financial Instability: Grant had times of financial instability, much like a lot of actors in their early careers. He had to take on a variety of odd jobs to sustain himself while pursuing his passion for performing due to the irregularity of acting gigs.

4. Handling Small Parts: Although Grant's early film and television roles—such as cameos in British TV shows like "The Last Place on Earth" (1985) and "Jenny's War" (1985)—were important for experience, they did not instantly result in significant successes. Even while these little parts gave him invaluable on-set experience, they

did not give him the exposure he needed to advance in his profession.

Initial Achievements

1. First Professional Breakthrough: In 1982, Grant landed his first role in a paid film, "Privileged," which was a student-produced movie supported by the Oxford Film Foundation. Despite its lackluster box office performance, the movie provided Grant with much-needed exposure and helped him build relationships in the business.

2. Breakthrough with "Maurice" (1987): James Ivory's film "Maurice," which starred Grant, was a major turning point in his career. Grant won praise from critics for his subtle portrayal of the young nobleman Clive Durham, who is struggling with his sexuality. Due to the film's success at the Venice Film Festival, where it took home the Silver Lion, Grant gained recognition as a serious actor who could play challenging characters.

Hugh Grant

3. Building Momentum: With appearances in movies like "The Lair of the White Worm" (1988) and "The Dawning" (1988), Grant maintained his momentum after the triumph of "Maurice." Even though they weren't huge hits, these movies demonstrated his adaptability and assisted him in developing a varied body of work.

4. "Four Weddings and a Funeral" (1994)
The role that Grant played Charles in "Four Weddings and a Funeral" was a turning point in his career. The movie was a huge hit, receiving positive reviews and rising to the top of the British box office at the time. Grant became well-known throughout the world and was awarded a Golden Globe for Best Actor for his role.

5. Recognition and Versatility: The popularity of "Four Weddings and a Funeral" made opportunities in romantic comedies and more somber dramas available to her. His roles in "Notting Hill" (1999) and "Sense and Sensibility" (1995) further cemented his standing as a multifaceted performer who can convey both charm and profundity.

Hugh Grant

Hugh Grant overcame his early difficulties—such as trouble landing jobs, unstable finances, and the possibility of being stereotyped—with tenacity and resolve. His early triumphs, especially his "Maurice" breakthrough and roles in movies like "Four Weddings and a Funeral," demonstrated his talent and adaptability and helped him become a major player in the film industry. Actors aiming to be like Grant are inspired by his narrative, which highlights the perseverance and hard work needed to succeed in the cutthroat business of performing.

Chapter 3: Ascent to Notoriety

A little bit of luck mixed with exceptional performances and timing propelled Hugh Grant to stardom. Grant's ascent to stardom is a monument to his talent and charisma, starting with his breakthrough performances and ending with his global recognition.

Notoriety and Financial Success

1. Honors and Nominations: For his roles in these movies, Grant was nominated for multiple honors and won multiple BAFTAs, Golden Globes, and Screen Actors Guild Awards. His reputation in the industry was cemented by his unwavering ability to captivate both reviewers and audiences.

2. Box Office Success: Grant became a bankable star thanks to the box office success of his films, several of which went on to become romantic comedy classics. His

films were highly successful at the box office, which made him one of the most sought-after actors of his era.

A string of memorable appearances in both critically acclaimed and financially successful films defined Hugh Grant's ascent to prominence. Grant's charisma, wit, and versatility endeared him to audiences worldwide, solidifying his status as a leading figure in the film industry and a beloved actor in the romantic comedy genre. His breakthrough performance in "Four Weddings and a Funeral" set the stage for a prolific career, with standout roles in "Sense and Sensibility," "Notting Hill," "Bridget Jones's Diary," and "About a Boy." His ascent to fame is evidence of his skill and timeless appeal.

Notable Hugh Grant Performances and Film

Hugh Grant's extensive career features a wide range of parts that highlight his flexibility as an actor. Throughout his multi-decade career, he has given standout performances in a variety of genres, including romantic

Hugh Grant

comedies and tragedies. Here are a few of his most important roles and movies:

"Maurice" (1987): "Clive Durham" in the role Summary: James Ivory's film "Maurice" is an adaptation of E.M. A young guy in early 20th-century England struggles with his sexuality in Forster's book.

Impact: Grant became a serious actor after receiving great acclaim for his nuanced portrayal of Clive Durham. He received a lot of attention after the film's Silver Lion win at the Venice Film Festival.

"Four Weddings and a Funeral" (1994) Part: "Charles" Synopsis: Mike Newell's romantic comedy tracks the journey of Charles and his companions through a string of marriages and a burial as they discover love and relationships.

Impact: Grant became well-known throughout the world and won a Golden Globe for Best Actor thanks to his lovable and engaging portrayal of Charles. Being a huge

Hugh Grant

hit at the box office, the movie went on to become one of the all-time biggest-grossing British movies.

Role: "Edward Ferrars" "Sense and Sensibility" (1995) Synopsis: Directed by Ang Lee, this Jane Austen adaptation follows the Dashwood sisters as they negotiate love and social expectations.

Impact: Grant's nuanced interpretation of Edward Ferrars demonstrated his deft handling of historical tragedies. With multiple accolades and critical acclaim, the movie improved Grant's standing even further.

"Notting Hill" (1999): "William Thacker" Synopsis: Roger Michell's romantic comedy centers on a London bookshop owner who develops feelings for Julia Roberts's character, a well-known American actress.

Impact: "Notting Hill" made about $363 million in revenue globally, making it a huge commercial success. Thanks to his portrayal of the endearing and sarcastic William Thacker, Grant won over fans all over the world.

Hugh Grant

The film "Bridget Jones's Diary" (2001) stars Sharon Maguire as Daniel Cleaver. It is based on Helen Fielding's novel, which follows Bridget Jones, a single woman juggling her personal and professional lives.

Impact: The film's love triangle became more intricate thanks to Grant's portrayal of the endearing yet roguish Daniel Cleaver. The film demonstrated Grant's ability to play against type and was a commercial hit.

"About a Boy" (2002), directed by Chris and Paul Weitz, stars Will Freeman in the title role. The story of Nick Hornby's novel, "About a Boy," centers on a carefree bachelor who develops an unexpected friendship with a young kid.

Impact: Grant showed off his range as an actor by portraying Will Freeman in a humorous and heartfelt way. The movie garnered positive reviews and expanded on Grant's body of work in the movies.

Hugh Grant

"Love Actually" (2003): "David, the Prime Minister" Synopsis: Richard Curtis's ensemble romantic comedy centers on several intertwined love stories set against the backdrop of Christmas.

Impact: One of the movie's greatest moments was Grant's portrayal of the affable Prime Minister, especially during his unforgettable dance sequence. "Love Actually" was a hit movie and is still a popular holiday favorite.

2016's "Florence Foster Jenkins": "St. Clair Bayfield Synopsis: Florence Foster Jenkins was an affluent socialite who, despite her lack of singing ability, aspired to be an opera singer. Her story is told in this Stephen Frears-directed film.

Impact: Grant received high appreciation for his portrayal as St. Clair Bayfield, Jenkins' dependable colleague, and was nominated for a BAFTA, Golden Globe, and Screen Actors Guild Award.

Hugh Grant

"Paddington 2" (2017): Playing the role of "Phoenix Buchanan" Synopsis: Paul King's family comedy centers on Paddington Bear's search for the thief who set him up for a crime.

Impact: Grant received critical acclaim and was a contender for a BAFTA for Best Supporting Actor for his outstanding depiction of the flamboyant and wicked Phoenix Buchanan.

Role: "Jeremy Thorpe" (2018) "A Very English Scandal" Synopsis: This BBC miniseries, directed by Stephen Frears, is based on the true story of British politician Jeremy Thorpe and the controversy that brought an end to his career.

Impact: Grant received high praise for his depiction of Jeremy Thorpe, which led to multiple nominations for awards and a Best Actor in a Leading Role BAFTA.

Hugh Grant's most notable roles and motion pictures showcase his extraordinary versatility and timeless appeal. From his early breakthrough in "Maurice" to his well-known parts in "Notting Hill," "Four Weddings and a Funeral," and "Bridget Jones's Diary," Grant has constantly wowed audiences with charming performances. His subsequent appearances in "Paddington 2," "Florence Foster Jenkins," and "A Very English Scandal" demonstrate his versatility and his ability to handle dramatic and humorous parts with equal skill.

Notable Partnerships with Co-Stars and Directors

Throughout his lengthy career, Hugh Grant has collaborated successfully on many projects with renowned directors and gifted co-stars. These collaborations have been crucial to his long-term career success and adaptability as an actor.

Directors

1. Mike Newell: "Four Weddings and a Funeral" (1994): Grant starred under Newell in this iconic romantic comedy, which marked a major career turning point and

was a huge hit. Grant's innate charisma and comedic timing were highlighted by their partnership, which won him a Golden Globe and propelled him to global renown.

2. Richard Curtis: "Notting Hill" (1999): Curtis was a key contributor to the development of William Thacker, one of Grant's most cherished characters. The movie's commercial success cemented Grant's place in the upper echelon of romantic comedies.

Grant starred as the charming Prime Minister in the ensemble romantic comedy "Love Actually" (2003), which Curtis directed. Their partnership produced one of the movie's most unforgettable scenes and helped ensure that it would always be remembered as a holiday classic.

3. Stephen Frears: "Florence Foster Jenkins" (2016): Under his direction, Grant's portrayal of St. Clair Bayfield demonstrated his comic and dramatic acting chops. Grant received a great deal of praise for the partnership and was nominated for numerous awards.

"A Very English Scandal" (2018): Under Frears' direction, Grant starred in this highly regarded BBC miniseries. He won multiple awards for his performance as Jeremy Thorpe, including a BAFTA for Best Actor in a Leading Role. This project showcased his range and nuance as an actor.

4. Paul King: "Paddington 2" (2017): A family comedy directed by Paul King, in which Grant portrayed the colorful villain Phoenix Buchanan. The movie won accolades from critics and garnered a nomination for a BAFTA for Best Supporting Actor for Grant's outstanding performance.

Co-stars

1. Julia Roberts: "Notting Hill" (1999): The popularity of the picture was largely due to Grant and Roberts's on-screen chemistry; their portrayal of a romantic relationship between a modest bookshop owner and a well-known actress struck a chord with viewers all over the world.

Renee Zellweger: "Bridget Jones's Diary" (2001): In this well-loved romantic comedy, Grant featured alongside

Hugh Grant

Zellweger; their relationship, together with Colin Firth's, established a captivating love triangle that became a distinguishing feature of the movie and its follow-ups.

2. "Bridget Jones: The Edge of Reason" (2004): Grant's Daniel Cleaver and Zellweger's Bridget Jones developed a deeper on-screen chemistry as the follow-up film further explored their complicated relationship.

3. Colin Firth: "Bridget Jones's Diary" (2001) and "Bridget Jones: The Edge of Reason" (2004): The antagonistic relationship between Grant and Colin Firth's character, Mark Darcy, brought a great deal of humor and drama to the movies. Their tense and humorous exchanges were some of the series' best moments.

4. "The Englishman Who Went Up a Hill But Came Down a Mountain" (1995): This comedy-drama also included Grant and Firth, demonstrating their relationship even more on screen.

Hugh Grant

5. Emma Thompson: Ang Lee directed "Sense and Sensibility" (1995), which starred Grant and Emma Thompson (who also authored the screenplay). Their teamwork produced a highly regarded movie that took home several honors, including the Academy Award for Best Adapted Screenplay.

Meryl Streep in "Florence Foster Jenkins" (2016): Meryl Streep and Grant had a highly acclaimed on-screen partnership that contributed significantly to the critical success of this biographical comedy-drama.

Hugh Grant's successful career has been greatly influenced by his noteworthy partnerships with co-stars like Julia Roberts, Renee Zellweger, Colin Firth, Emma Thompson, and Meryl Streep, as well as his collaborations with directors like Mike Newell, Richard Curtis, Stephen Frears, and Paul King. These partnerships have allowed Grant to demonstrate his depth, charm, and versatility as an actor, which has added to his lasting appeal and legacy in the film industry.

Hugh Grant

Recognitions and Submissions

Hugh Grant's career has been marked by a multitude of nominations and awards, which is indicative of his success in both the film and critic communities. A few of his noteworthy honors are as follows:

1. Golden Globe Awards: Grant has been nominated several times for previous performances and has won a Golden Globe for Best Actor in a Motion Picture, Musical, or Comedy for "Four Weddings and a Funeral".

2. BAFTA Awards: He has been nominated for multiple parts and has won a BAFTA for Best Actor in a Leading Role for "A Very English Scandal".

3. Screen Actors Guild Awards: Grant is a multiple-time nominee for the SAG Awards, having starred in "Florence Foster Jenkins."

Grant has received a nomination for a Primetime Emmy Award because of his work in "A Very English Scandal."

Hugh Grant

Hugh Grant's career has been marked by both critical and commercial success. He has won over audiences and critics with his performances in films such as "About a Boy," "Notting Hill," "Four Weddings and a Funeral," and "Bridget Jones's Diary." More recently, he has shown his talent and versatility in roles like "Florence Foster Jenkins" and "A Very English Scandal." Having worked in the film industry for several decades, Grant is still a beloved and significant figure in the industry.

Chapter 4: Characterizing Hugh Grant in Classic Movies

Here's a detailed look at Hugh Grant's performances in "Four Weddings and a Funeral," "Notting Hill," "Bridget Jones's Diary," and "Love Actually"—a few of the classic roles that have defined his career and solidified his legacy as a renowned actor.

Approach and Style of Acting

Hugh Grant's signature charm is evident in roles like Charles in "Four Weddings and a Funeral" and William Thacker in "Notting Hill." His characters are flawed yet endearing, drawing audiences in with their wit and charisma. Hugh Grant frequently embodies characters who exude a charming and affable persona, which becomes a central aspect of his performances.

Hugh Grant

Example: Grant's portrayal of Charles in "Four Weddings and a Funeral" is characterized by his easy charm and comedic timing. He imbues the character with a relatable awkwardness that makes Charles endearing and relatable. Grant's ability to strike a balance between humor and emotional depth enables him to capture the complexities of relationships and love.

1. Realistic and Relatable Characters: Grant's performances are based on a naturalistic style that enables viewers to relate to the characters on a personal level. He frequently creates characters that feel genuine and relatable, despite their occasionally larger-than-life circumstances.

Example: William Thacker in "Notting Hill" Grant takes a more reflective and subtle approach to his portrayal of William Thacker than he did in "Four Weddings and a Funeral," highlighting the character's goals and daily challenges. The audience is moved by Grant's ability to be genuine and authentic in his performance, which makes William's path of self-discovery engrossing and moving.

2. Humor and Comic Timing: In many of his performances, especially romantic comedies, where he shines at delivering sharp dialogue and interacting with humorous circumstances, Grant's comedic instincts and timing are essential.

Example: Daniel Cleaver in "Bridget Jones's Diary" Grant's portrayal of Daniel Cleaver is marked by his sharp wit and playful demeanor. He provides a mischievous charm to the role, making Daniel both seductive and unpredictable. Grant's ability to strike a balance between humor and underlying complexity gives the character depth and makes his interactions with co-stars, such as Renee Zellweger's Bridget Jones, compelling.

3. Emotional Depth and Vulnerability: In addition to his humorous abilities, Grant's acting demonstrates emotional depth and vulnerability, which let him delve

Hugh Grant

into the nuanced inner lives and interpersonal dynamics of his characters.

Example: Prime Minister David in "Love Actually" Grant's portrayal of Prime Minister David exemplifies his ability to blend humor with real emotion; he sensitively and sincerely depicts David's transformation from political leader to lovesick romantic, capturing the character's internal struggles and personal development to create moments that audiences will remember.

Hugh Grant is a celebrated figure in romantic comedies and beyond. His enduring appeal lies in his ability to balance comedic flair with genuine emotion, creating characters that are both memorable and relatable on screen. His acting style is defined by a blend of charm, humor, emotional depth, and naturalistic portrayal of characters. Across iconic films like "Four Weddings and a Funeral," "Notting Hill," "Bridget Jones's Diary," and "Love Actually," Grant consistently demonstrates his versatility and ability to bring complex characters to life.

Chapter 5: Private Life

Hugh Grant

Throughout his career, Hugh Grant's personal life has been a subject of attention due to his significant partnerships and his transition into fatherhood. The following is a summary of his family and relationships:

Connections

1. Elizabeth Hurley (1987–2000): Elizabeth Hurley, a British actress and model, was the most well-known partner of Hugh Grant. The two became one of the most celebrity couples of the 1990s, and their relationship lasted for more than ten years, marked by their glamorous appearances together at red carpet events and premieres. Hurley helped Grant through many career turning points, including the early successes of movies like "Four Weddings and a Funeral" and "Notting Hill." Despite their high-profile status, the couple faced difficulties, especially following Grant's 1995 arrest in Los Angeles, which damaged their public image but did not immediately result in a breakup. In 2000, they formally separated but remained friends, with Hurley continuing to speak at events.

Hugh Grant

2. Jemima Khan (2004–2007): After splitting from Hurley, Grant started dating British–Pakistani journalist and activist Jemima Khan. Because of Khan's social standing and Grant's celebrity, their romance attracted a lot of media attention. Throughout their relationship, which lasted from 2004 to 2007, they were frequently spotted together at various public events and social gatherings. Khan's presence and support gave Grant a sense of stability in the face of constant media scrutiny.

3. Tinglan Hong and Fatherhood: In 2011, Hugh Grant's personal life took a dramatic turn when it was revealed that he had become a father for the first time. He had been dating Tinglan Hong, a Chinese receptionist, and his daughter, Tabitha Grant, was born in September of that year. Given Grant's prior public views on marriage and fatherhood, many were taken aback by the news, but Grant embraced fatherhood with gusto and later described it as a life-changing experience.

Just a few months after Tabitha was born, in 2012, Grant and Tinglan Hong received their second child, a son

Hugh Grant

called John Mungo Grant. John Mungo's arrival reinforced Grant's dedication to parenthood, as he took an active role in raising his kids while juggling his profession.

Hugh Grant and Anna Eberstein have a long-standing and private relationship that started in 2012. Eberstein is a Swedish television producer who has supported Hugh Grant in both personal and professional endeavors. In 2018, Grant and Eberstein celebrated their marriage in a private ceremony, which was a significant turning point in their relationship. Their marriage shows how Grant has changed his views on marriage and family life and how committed he is to providing a stable and loving environment for their children.

4. Fatherhood and Parenting: Hugh Grant's experience as a father has changed his priorities and personal life. He used to be hesitant to get married and have kids, but he has embraced his role as a father with passion and hard work. His parenting style shows that he wants to give his

kids stability, love, and guidance, but he also values their privacy in the face of public scrutiny.

Significant relationships—such as his high-profile romances with Elizabeth Hurley and Jemima Khan, as well as his journey into parenthood with Tinglan Hong and Anna Eberstein—have shaped Hugh Grant's outlook on life and shaped his public persona as a gifted actor and loving family man. Grant's ability to balance the demands of celebrity with his sense of privacy and authenticity highlights his dedication to personal development and happiness.

Hugh Grant's career has seen a great deal of change in his public persona and media coverage due to his acting roles, personal experiences, and press encounters.

Hugh Grant

Public perception and media attention

1. Early Career and Romantic Comedy Persona: Hugh Grant gained international recognition in the early 1990s for his roles in romantic comedies like "Four Weddings and a Funeral" and "Notting Hill." His pleasant and witty on-screen persona as an Englishman made him a leading figure in the genre, and his capacity to portray likable but flawed characters won him over fans and cemented his reputation as a gifted actor with a knack for comedic timing.

2. Controversies and Image Challenges: Despite his success, Hugh Grant had a major public image problem in 1995 after he was arrested in Los Angeles for having sex with a prostitute. The incident was widely reported in the media and had the potential to ruin his career. Grant later apologized in public and offered a sincere apology, as well as an honest admission of guilt and regret. Although the scandal damaged his reputation for

Hugh Grant

a while, the public and media accepted his sincere apology and his subsequent efforts to mend his reputation.

Hugh Grant's use of satire and self-deprecating humor has been a recurring theme throughout his career. He has made witty and candid remarks in interviews, poking fun at his persona as a charming but occasionally bumbling Englishman. This approach has won him over fans and helped to shape a public image of someone who doesn't take himself too seriously, despite the challenges of fame and media scrutiny.

Hugh Grant has been a strong advocate for press reform and stricter regulations to protect individuals' privacy rights, particularly in light of the phone hacking scandal involving the British tabloid News of the World. His advocacy efforts have earned him respect beyond his acting career and demonstrate his commitment to ethical journalism and accountability in media practices. 4. Privacy Concerns and Media Intrusion: Hugh Grant has

Hugh Grant

been a vocal critic of media intrusion and privacy invasion.

3. Political Engagement and Social Commentary: Hugh Grant has been actively involved in political activism and social commentary on a variety of issues outside of his acting career. He has been vocal about his opposition to Brexit and has backed campaigns for social justice and environmental conservation. Grant's willingness to use his public platform to advocate for causes he believes in has further improved his reputation as a politically engaged and socially conscious person.

Hugh Grant's public persona has changed throughout his career from that of a romantic comedy star to that of a respected actor and social activist for causes such as ethical journalism and social justice. Despite obstacles in his path, Grant has always maintained a genuine sense of humor and authenticity that connects with viewers. His ability to handle the spotlight with grace and his unwavering dedication to morality and social responsibility have further shaped his public persona as a gifted performer and a responsible member of society.

A closer look at some of these significant events that have defined Hugh Grant's journey in Hollywood and beyond can be found here. Hugh Grant's life and career have been marked by personal trials and triumphs:

Individual Difficulties

1. The Los Angeles Arrest and Public Scrutiny: Hugh Grant faced a great deal of public scrutiny and criticism following his arrest in 1995 for engaging in lewd conduct with a sex worker. This event sparked a media frenzy and put his budding career as a leading romantic comedy actor in jeopardy. Consequently, Grant underwent a period of introspection and personal development.

2. Image Rehabilitation and Apology: Hugh Grant proactively worked to repair his reputation and win back the public's trust following his arrest. He publicly expressed regret for his actions, acknowledged the

negative effects they had on his career and personal life, and apologized for his behavior. Grant's sincere apology and dedication to taking responsibility for his actions were key factors in reducing the scandal's aftermath and helped him gain respect for his integrity and humility.

Career Accomplishments

1. Career Resurgence and Versatility: Hugh Grant overcame difficult circumstances early in his career to attain a remarkable Hollywood comeback, demonstrating his range and talent in dramatic and character-driven roles that went beyond romantic comedies. Movies like "Florence Foster Jenkins," "Paddington 2," and the highly regarded miniseries "A Very English Scandal" showcased Grant's ability to captivate audiences with nuanced performances.

2. Awards and Recognition: Hugh Grant's achievements in the film industry have been reinforced by recognition and awards from the industry. He has been nominated for and won multiple awards, including the Screen Actors

Hugh Grant

Guild Awards, the Golden Globe Awards, and BAFTA nominations. His ability to switch between dramatic and comedic roles has cemented his place as one of the industry's most respected and admired actors.

3. Fatherhood and Family Life: Despite early misgivings about getting married and starting a family early in his career, Hugh Grant embraced fatherhood with passion and dedication. He has children from relationships with Tinglan Hong and Anna Eberstein, actively involved in their upbringing and savoring the joys of parenthood. Hugh Grant has talked warmly about the transformative impact of fatherhood on his life, emphasizing the fulfillment and joy it has brought him. These are some of his most profound personal triumphs.

4. Advocacy and Social Impact: Hugh Grant has not only used his public platform to entertain audiences but also to champion causes that he believes in. In the wake of the British tabloid phone hacking scandal, he has been a vocal supporter of press reform and privacy rights, and his attempts to hold the media responsible for immoral

Hugh Grant

behavior have sparked broader conversations about media ethics and the defense of people's privacy.

Hugh Grant's life has been shaped by both personal setbacks that tested his fortitude and morality and victories that highlighted his brilliance and honesty. From navigating public

Chapter 5: Career Development

Hugh Grant's career has been an interesting path from the success of romantic comedies to roles that are somber and intricate. This change demonstrates his adaptability as an actor and his capacity for self-reinvention. This is a comprehensive examination of Hugh Grant's effective move into more serious parts and the growth of his acting career.

First Moves in the Direction of Dramatic Roles

With jobs that alluded to his breadth as an actor, Grant started to move away from his romantic comedy persona. Among the early forays into many genres are:

(2002) "About a Boy": Grant, as conceited bachelor Will Freeman who develops an improbable bond with a tiny child, struck a mix between comedy and a more profoundly emotional story. His ability to manage more complicated roles without losing his charm was demonstrated in this role.

"Music and Lyrics" (2007): Grant showed hints of his dramatic talent as a washed-up pop singer who had to explore themes of self-discovery and atonement, even if the film remained a romantic comedy.

In the 2010s, Grant began to play more serious parts, taking on roles that required a higher level of emotional nuance and complexity.

"Cloud Atlas" (2012) Part: Various Personas Overview: Grant plays several parts in several eras and plots in this grandiose science fiction epic helmed by the Wachowskis and Tom Tykwer. He was able to demonstrate his versatility in this movie, playing anything from a future tribal chief to a cunning hotel manager.

Hugh Grant

Impact: "Cloud Atlas" was a notable departure from Grant's customary repertoire, showcasing his versatility in taking on unusual and different parts.

The 2016 film "Florence Foster Jenkins" St. Clair Bayfield's role Summary: In this Stephen Frears-directed biographical comedy-drama, Meryl Streep and Grant play the husband and actor of Florence Foster Jenkins, a New York socialite who loves to sing despite her lack of skill.

Impact: Grant's sensitive and nuanced portrayal won plaudits for demonstrating his ability to strike a balance between comedy and emotional complexity. He was nominated for many awards for his performance, including Best Actor in a Supporting Role at the BAFTAs.

(2017) "Paddington 2" Participant: Phoenix Buchanan Synopsis: Grant portrays a former actor who went bad and becomes Paddington Bear's adversary in this family-friendly adventure-comedy.

Hugh Grant

Impact: Grant received significant praise for his depiction of Phoenix Buchanan, which emphasized his comic timing and dramatic flair. His performance was regarded as one of the movie's highlights and helped it become successful both critically and commercially.

The 2018 film "A Very English Scandal" Jeremy Thorpe in the role Synopsis: Based on the actual story of British politician Jeremy Thorpe, who was prosecuted and found not guilty of plotting to kill his former girlfriend in the 1970s, this television miniseries directed by Stephen Frears tells his narrative.

Impact: Grant's depiction of Jeremy Thorpe was a dramatic shift from his earlier parts, demonstrating his command of the theater and his capacity to inhabit a nuanced, ethically gray character. He received positive reviews for the role and was nominated for many awards, including a Golden Globe for Best Actor in a Miniseries or Television Film.

Hugh Grant

Industry Recognition and Critical Acclaim

Both the film industry and critics have praised Hugh Grant for his seamless move into more serious parts. His roles in TV shows and movies have shown how adaptable he is and how he can take on difficult and varied roles. This development has increased his attractiveness and cemented his place in the industry as a reputable and well-liked actor.

Hugh Grant's career is still developing and changing as he takes on more challenging and varied tasks. His longevity in the business has been guaranteed by his willingness to venture outside of his comfort zone and investigate other genres and character types. Both admirers and detractors are interested in seeing how he will continue to push the limits of his skill in upcoming endeavors.

Hugh Grant

Hugh Grant's transformation from a romantic comedy star to a multifaceted performer with the capacity to create potent tragic performances demonstrates his artistic growth and versatility. He has gained critical recognition and respect in the business by showcasing his range and depth in more serious parts. Grant's career is proof of his skill and commitment to the film industry, solidifying his status as a revered personality.

Notable Later Motion Pictures and TV Series

Several noteworthy movies and television shows that showcase Hugh Grant's adaptability and ongoing significance in the entertainment business define his latter career. Here are a few of his most well-known recent pieces:

In the 2016 film "Florence Foster Jenkins" St. Clair Bayfield's role Stephen Frears is the director. Summary: Meryl Streep portrays Florence Foster Jenkins, a New York socialite who loves to sing despite her lack of skill, in this biographical comedy-drama. Hugh Grant portrays St. Clair Bayfield, her manager and spouse, who is committed to shielding her from the unpleasant realities of her vocal prowess.

Impact: The depth of passion and humorous timing in Grant's performance was highly appreciated. His performance as Bayfield gave the movie a touch of sensitivity and nuance, and it led to nominations for honors including the BAFTA for Best Actor in a Supporting Role.

(2017) "Paddington 2" Participant: Phoenix Buchanan Paul King is the director. The plot of this family adventure-comedy revolves around Paddington Bear, who goes to purchase his aunt Lucy a special pop-up book for her birthday only to have it stolen. The antagonist of the movie, Phoenix Buchanan, played by Grant, is a broken actor who is out to steal the book for himself.

Hugh Grant

Impact: Grant received high praise for his portrayal, which demonstrated his versatility in playing a flashy and humorous villain. In addition to helping the movie achieve critical and economic success, his depiction of Buchanan was exceptional and earned him a nomination for a BAFTA for Best Supporting Actor.

In the 2018 film "A Very English Scandal" Jeremy Thorpe in the role of Stephen Frears is the director. The synopsis of this television miniseries says that it is based on the actual story of British politician Jeremy Thorpe, who was put on trial for planning to kill Norman Scott, his former lover. In his portrayal of Thorpe, Grant successfully conveys the character's dark complexity, charm, and ambition.

Impact: Grant's depiction of Jeremy Thorpe demonstrated his dramatic breadth and capacity to represent individuals with conflicting moral convictions, marking a substantial shift from his earlier portrayals. Grant's work in the series won him many nominations for awards, including a Golden Globe nomination for

Hugh Grant

Best Actor in a Miniseries or Television Film. The series was well-received by critics.

In 2019, "The Gentlemen" Position: Fletcher Guy Ritchie is the director. The film's synopsis centers on Mickey Pearson (played by Matthew McConaughey), an American expat who manages a lucrative marijuana business in London. In the film, Grant portrays Fletcher, a cunning private eye who attempts to blackmail Pearson.

Impact: Grant was able to explore a darker and more humorous persona in his portrayal of Fletcher, which was a change from his usual performances. His performance gave the movie a humorous and intriguing element that enhanced its overall appeal.

In 2020, in "The Undoing" Jonathan Fraser in the role Susanne Bier is the director. Summary: Hugh Grant and Nicole Kidman play married couple Jonathan and Grace Fraser in this HBO drama. Their lives are drastically altered when Jonathan's startling secrets are unearthed

Hugh Grant

during a murder investigation. Grant plays an endearing doctor whose troubled history is revealed.

Impact: Grant's critically lauded performance in "The Undoing" demonstrated his ability to depict a complicated character subtly and intriguingly. He was nominated for many accolades, including a Golden Globe for Best Actor in a Miniseries or Television Film, for his role in the series.

Hugh Grant made a successful transition to playing characters that were more complicated and varied, as seen by his notable later films and television work. Grant has always shown his flexibility and aptitude as an actor, appearing in everything from crime flicks and psychological thrillers to family comedies and biographical dramas. His ongoing reputation as a respected figure in the entertainment business has been cemented by his ability to embrace a wide range of personas and genres.

Hugh Grant

Input toward Film Production

Hugh Grant has had a renowned acting career in addition to a noteworthy career as a film producer. His behind-the-scenes employment has allowed him to encourage up-and-coming talent in the business and have an impact on the creative direction of projects. An outline of his accomplishments as a film producer is shown below:

In the late 1990s and early 2000s, Hugh Grant started his career as a film producer. His early attempts were driven by a desire to experiment more with filming techniques and assume greater creative control.

In 1999, "Mickey Blue Eyes" Function: Executive Producer and Actor Summary: In this romantic comedy, Hugh Grant plays Englishman Michael Felgate, who gets involved with the Mafia after proposing to his fiancee, whose father is a crime leader. Grant was able to have a big impact on the creation and execution of the movie because of his role as executive producer.

Hugh Grant

Impact: Despite not being a huge box office hit, the movie demonstrated Grant's versatility as an actor by combining his acting and producing duties. This was a significant step in his career diversification.

The 2001 book "Bridget Jones's Diary" Function: Executive Producer and Actor Synopsis: This movie, which is based on Helen Fielding's novel, centers on Renée Zellweger's character Bridget Jones, a single woman in London who struggles to balance her professional and romantic relationships. In addition to acting as an executive producer, Grant portrayed the endearing but imperfect Daniel Cleaver.

Impact: The movie was a huge box office and critical success. Because of his combined responsibilities as producer and performer, Grant was able to add to the overall creative concept of the movie and solidify its reputation as a popular romantic comedy.

Hugh Grant

As a producer, Grant has frequently taken a calculated approach, concentrating on projects that have distinctive storytelling chances or that fit with his artistic pursuits.

"The Rewrite" (2014) Function: Executive Producer and Actor Summary: Grant plays a broken-hearted screenwriter in this romantic comedy, where he finds inspiration and a fresh perspective on life after accepting a teaching position at a tiny university. He was able to influence the story and production style of the movie in his capacity as executive producer.

Impact: Despite not seeing much box office success, many enjoyed the movie for its endearing and lovable narrative. Grant's participation as a producer demonstrated his dedication to works with rich characters and compelling storylines.

Hugh Grant

Fostering Innovative Projects and Up-and-Coming Talent

Beyond his leading parts, Grant has demonstrated that he is a keen supporter of up-and-coming talent and creative endeavors in the business.

In 2019, "The Gentlemen" Part: Associate Producer and Actor Overview: In this Guy Ritchie-directed criminal comedy, Grant plays the unscrupulous private investigator Fletcher, a departure from his usual characters. As an associate producer, Grant supported Ritchie's idea for a chic and captivating story by contributing to the film's conception and production.

Impact: "The Gentlemen" was well-received both critically and commercially, mostly due to Grant's outstanding performance and producing credits. His participation proved that he could work well with other filmmakers to foster creative narrative.

Hugh Grant

Beyond his playing career, Hugh Grant's impact on the entertainment business has grown thanks to his work as a film producer. His willingness to embrace a variety of projects and assume more creative control has demonstrated his adaptability and dedication to storytelling. Grant has shown a deep grasp of the filmmaking process and a commitment to bringing fascinating tales to life by juggling his jobs as an actor and producer. His contributions behind the scenes have shaped his reputation as a complex and significant character in film history.

Chapter 6: Honors and Commendations

Hugh Grant has received several honors and nominations during his career, acknowledging his skill, adaptability, and achievements in the motion picture and television industries. An outline of some of the significant honors and nominations he has gotten is provided below:

Golden Globe Awards: "Four Weddings and a Funeral" won Best Actor in a Motion Picture Musical or Comedy after receiving several nominations.

BAFTA Awards: "Four Weddings and a Funeral" won Best Actor in a Leading Role after receiving several nominations.

Multiple nominations for the Screen Actors Guild Awards, including two for Outstanding Performance by a Cast and Individual Performance.

Hugh Grant

Critics' Choice Awards: He received nominations for his roles in television and movies, which demonstrated his adaptability and garnered positive reviews.

Recipient of the European Film Awards: Honored for "Four Weddings and a Funeral."

Hugh Grant has received constant appreciation from critics for his ability to strike a balance between comedy and passion, his effortless on-screen persona, and his willingness to take on a variety of difficult parts.

Versatility: It is often known that Grant can effortlessly switch from romantic comedies to dramatic and character-driven parts. His versatility and breadth have been demonstrated by his roles in movies such as "A Very English Scandal," "Paddington 2," and "Florence Foster Jenkins."

Depth and complexity: Grant's ability to give his characters depth and complexity has been praised by critics for making them likable and compelling. His representations are unique and powerful because they frequently combine charm and depth.

Comic Timing: Grant's comic timing is well-known, and he has made a name for himself in lighter parts and romantic comedies. He has won over both reviewers and fans with his effortless delivery of physical humor and clever language.

Hugh Grant's acting career is proof of his skill and adaptability. His early triumphs in romantic comedies served as a springboard for a varied and well-regarded body of work. He has received plaudits from critics and the business for his willingness to try new things and take on difficult jobs. Hugh Grant is a well-known character in the entertainment business who never fails to enthrall audiences and reviewers with his performances, cementing his reputation as a brilliant and versatile actor.

Chapter 7: Activism and Philanthropy

Hugh Grant is well-known for his noteworthy contributions to activism and philanthropy in addition to his storied acting career. He has actively supported several philanthropic causes and organizations throughout the years, leveraging his position to bring about constructive change. Here is a thorough examination of his advocacy and charitable endeavors.

Charitable Activities and Issues Hugh Grant Endorses

Hugh Grant has devoted a large amount of his time and finances to helping many nonprofits and causes. His varied charitable endeavors demonstrate his dedication to several social causes, including children's welfare, press reform, healthcare, and education. Here is a

Hugh Grant

summary of the causes and philanthropic endeavors he is actively involved in:

1. Healthcare and Medical Research: Hugh Grant has demonstrated great dedication to causes relating to healthcare, especially those that address uncommon diseases, dementia, and terminal illnesses.

- Marie Curie: Grant has long supported the nonprofit organization Marie Curie, which offers assistance and care to those with terminal diseases. His participation has aided in increasing awareness of the cause and money for the organization's nursing and hospice services.

- Dementia UK: Grant supports Dementia UK, which provides specialized dementia assistance through Admiral Nurses, in remembrance of his mother, who suffered from dementia. His work has brought attention to the difficulties experienced by relatives of dementia patients as well as the value of caregiver assistance.

Hugh Grant

- Fynvola Foundation: Grant has donated to this nonprofit organization that assists adults with learning difficulties. His assistance has made it easier to provide people with complicated needs with high-quality care and services.

2. Children's Welfare and Education: Grant's dedication to raising the next generation is evident in his enthusiasm for enhancing the lives of kids and funding educational programs.

- The Felix Project: This nonprofit fights food poverty by salvaging extra food and giving it to educational institutions and charitable organizations. With Grant's assistance, needy children and families have been able to get wholesome meals, enhancing food security and cutting down on waste.

- Small Steps Project: Grant has contributed to this initiative, which helps kids who live in trash dumps all around the world. To help these kids take a step toward a better future, the organization provides food, shoes, and education.

- Support for Refugee Crisis: Grant has made donations to groups that aid in the relocation of refugees and asylum seekers, with a particular emphasis on giving displaced children and families who are victims of persecution and war vital supplies.

3. Advocacy for Press Reform: Grant has become a strong voice for press reform and privacy protection as a result of his own experiences with media intrusion.

- Hacked Off Campaign: Grant is a well-known backer of this initiative, which calls for a press that is both independent and responsible. The campaign emphasizes the need for more regulation and accountability while working to safeguard people from press abuse and uphold ethical standards in journalism.

- Leveson Inquiry: Grant testified in the Leveson Inquiry on his experiences with phone hacking and press harassment, and he played a significant part in the investigation. His participation contributed to raising awareness of the necessity for changes in media policies and the defense of people's right to privacy.

4. Support for the Arts: Grant's philanthropic donations to institutions devoted to safeguarding and advancing cultural landmarks and creative pursuits are evidence of his passion for the arts.

- Theatres Trust: Grant contributes to this charitable organization, which aims to preserve and advance theaters throughout the United Kingdom. His efforts have supported the arts and promoted cultural enrichment by assisting in the preservation of significant cultural institutions.

5. Participation in Fundraising Events: Grant has used his platform to generate money and awareness for several charity organizations by taking part in several fundraising events and making public appearances.

Hugh Grant

- Comic Relief: Grant regularly contributes to Comic Relief, a well-known UK charity that fights social injustice and poverty. He has participated in telethons and fundraising activities, which have helped the organization raise a sizable sum of money for its projects both domestically and abroad.

- Great Ormond Street Hospital: Grant has assisted in the fundraising efforts for this renowned London children's hospital. His donations have aided in providing extremely sick children with essential medical treatment and research funding.

6. Environmental and Animal Welfare: In line with his larger dedication to sustainability and compassion for all living things, Grant has also demonstrated support for causes about the environment and animal welfare.

- Save the Children: This organization tackles environmental concerns that affect children's health and well-being, even though its primary concentration is on children. Grant's assistance to this organization goes toward funding programs designed to safeguard kids' futures in the face of climate change.

- Wildlife Conservation: Grant has made donations to several organizations that help the preservation of endangered animals and their natural environments. His contributions support conservation efforts and increase public understanding of the value of biodiversity.

Hugh Grant's many humanitarian endeavors show his dedication to improving society and his support for a variety of causes. His charitable endeavors, which range from press reform and the arts to healthcare and children's welfare, are a true testament to his sense of duty and compassion. Grant has cemented his reputation as a gifted actor and devoted humanitarian by using his talents and position to serve those in need and bring about significant change.

Hugh Grant

Activism in Politics and Society

In addition to being a skilled actor, Hugh Grant is a vocal supporter of politics and social causes. Throughout the years, he has demonstrated his dedication to advancing justice, accountability, and fairness by using his position to speak out on a variety of topics, including press freedom and election reform. An outline of his social and political involvement is provided below:

1. Press Reform and Media Accountability: Fighting for press reform and media accountability is one of Grant's most important areas of action. His zeal for promoting ethical journalism and standing up for victims of press malpractice has been stoked by his encounters with intrusive media tactics.

- Hacked Off Campaign: Grant is a prominent member of this movement that supports an open and responsible press. The campaign was started in reaction to the phone hacking incident and was designed to shield people from mistreatment by the press and make sure that journalists followed moral guidelines. Grant's participation has been essential in igniting the media reform debate and increasing public awareness.

- Leveson Inquiry: A judicial public investigation of the customs, procedures, and morality of the British press, Grant was a key player in this investigation. His statement on his encounters with press harassment and phone hacking brought to light the necessity of strict laws and the defense of people's right to privacy. Grant's remarks influenced the proposals for press reform made by the panel.

2. Electoral Reform: Grant has also made a strong case for the necessity of a more equitable and representative voting process in the United Kingdom.

- Support for Proportional Representation: Grant has contributed to efforts in favor of proportional representation, a voting scheme designed to guarantee that a party's win of seats corresponds to the number of votes it earned. He has campaigned for a system that more accurately represents the will of the people, contending that the existing first-past-the-post system is antiquated and results in unequal representation.

- Pushing for Tactical Voting: To keep the Conservative Party from winning a majority, Grant has advocated for tactical voting in prior elections. To advance a more representative and equal parliament, he has urged people to back candidates who, regardless of their party membership, have the highest chance of unseating Conservative incumbents.

3. Human Rights and Social Justice: Grant's activity encompasses a wider range of human rights and social justice concerns, which is indicative of his dedication to promoting the interests of underprivileged and susceptible populations.

- Support for Refugees: Grant has contributed to organizations that assist refugees and asylum seekers and has been a steadfast advocate for refugee rights. His campaigning has brought attention to the predicament of internally displaced people and the significance of offering safety and humanitarian aid to those escaping persecution and violence.

- LGBTQ+ Rights: Grant has openly endorsed LGBTQ+ rights and taken part in movements calling for nondiscrimination and equality. His dedication to advancing justice and inclusion for all people, regardless of their sexual orientation or gender identity, is demonstrated by his support of LGBTQ+ initiatives.

4. Environmental Advocacy: Grant's support of sustainability and the preservation of natural resources is evident in his environmental advocacy. He has backed several programs that combat climate change and encourage environmental preservation.

- assistance for Environmental Charities: Grant has made contributions to and provided assistance for organizations that preserve natural areas, save endangered species, and advance sustainable lifestyles. His donations support vital conservation initiatives and

Hugh Grant

increase public understanding of the value of environmental stewardship.

- Awareness of Climate Change: Grant has made use of his position to spread the word about the effects of climate change and the pressing need for action. He has included the need for sustainable solutions and climate change in the global conversation by endorsing environmental campaigns and projects.

Hugh Grant's commitment to promoting justice, accountability, and fairness in a variety of contexts is demonstrated by his political and social involvement. His activities demonstrate a strong dedication to having a beneficial social influence, ranging from press reform and electoral justice to environmental protection and human rights. Through the use of his riches and public platform, Grant has supported projects that uphold moral principles, safeguard marginalized communities, and guarantee a more equitable and sustainable future. His status as a socially conscious and involved public person

Hugh Grant

is further cemented by the fact that his advocacy still motivates and propels significant change.

Chapter 8: Legacy and Effects

With a career spanning more than three decades, Hugh Grant has made a lasting impression on both popular culture and the film business. Renowned for his charisma, humor, and adaptability, Grant has influenced romantic comedies and other genres. Here's a closer look at his impact:

Reimagining the Romantic Comedy

In the 1990s and early 2000s, Hugh Grant is frequently credited with reinventing the romantic comedy subgenre. His parts in classic movies delivered a distinct fusion of charm, comedy, and vulnerability that redefined the norm for romantic leads.

Hugh Grant

- Grant's depiction of Charles, an endearing but clumsy Englishman, in "Four Weddings and a Funeral" (1994) served as a model for romantic comedy heroes. The success of the movie launched him to global fame and brought new life to the genre, inspiring a plethora of follow-up productions.

- "Notting Hill" (1999): Grant solidified his reputation as the archetypal romantic lead by portraying William Thacker, a modest bookstore owner who falls in love with a well-known actress. The movie's financial success and ongoing appeal demonstrated his capacity to emotionally connect with viewers.

- "Bridget Jones's Diary" (2001): Grant demonstrated his versatility as the roguish Daniel Cleaver by fusing charm with a hint of villainy. His portrayal gave the role more nuance and enhanced the movie's critical and financial reception, therefore cementing his legacy as a romantic comedy star.

Hugh Grant

Increasing to Dramatic Positions

Grant's shift to more dramatic parts showcased his range as an actor and helped him become more well-known than just a romantic comedy star.

- "About a Boy" (2002): Grant won praise all over for his portrayal of Will Freeman, a conceited bachelor who discovers compassion. He gained more recognition in the profession because of the part, which demonstrated his ability to manage complicated characters and plots.

- 2016's in the role of St "Florence Foster Jenkins": Clair Bayfield, Grant demonstrated his ability to handle drama while keeping his humorous timing. He received many award nominations for the part, which demonstrated his ability to strike a balance between comedy and emotional nuance.

"A Very English Scandal" (2018): Praised as one of Grant's best roles, the film followed Jeremy Thorpe, a British politician caught up in a controversy. He received several honors and critical acclaim for the part, which showed that he could play serious and complex characters.

Input to the British Film Industry

Hugh Grant's popularity has had a significant influence on British cinema, drawing notice to British movies and directors on a global scale.

- Working Title Films: This production company produced several of Grant's best-known movies, including "Notting Hill," "Four Weddings and a Funeral," and "Bridget Jones's Diary." His partnerships with this production firm have greatly enhanced its standing and prosperity.

- Fostering the Careers of Other Actors and Directors: Many British actors have found their start in and success as a result of Grant's films, which frequently include ensembles of gifted performers. His collaborations with filmmakers such as Stephen Frears and Richard Curtis

Hugh Grant

have brought attention to British filmmaking talent on a worldwide scale.

Popularity and Cultural Impact

Hugh Grant has become a legendary character in popular culture, influencing things outside the realm of film.

- Famous Characters and Quotable Phrases: With catchy words and moments that still make an impact on viewers, Grant's appearances in movies like "Notting Hill" and "Four Weddings and a Funeral" have left a lasting legacy. His characters are frequently brought up in conversations about vintage romantic comedies.

- Sarcastically Funny Appearances: Grant's propensity to make lighthearted jokes about himself has won him over to fans. He has done this in the films "Music and Lyrics" (2007) and the 2020 series "The Undoing," among other shows.

Hugh Grant

Accomplishments and Nominations: Throughout his career, Grant has been recognized with several honors and nominations, such as a Screen Actors Guild Award, a BAFTA, and a Golden Globe. These honors are a testament to his brilliance and the importance of his contributions.

Hugh Grant's successful crossover to serious parts, the inventiveness of the romantic comedy genre, and noteworthy contributions to British filmmaking have had a lasting impression on both the film business and popular culture. Audiences throughout the world have been profoundly impacted by his endearing, subtle performances. In addition to his acting abilities, Grant's readiness to participate in political and social activity and push for press reform strengthens his reputation as a significant and well-liked person. His work assures his position in cinematic history by inspiring and entertaining us even now.

Hugh Grant

Views from Critics and Peers

Both reviewers and his fellow members of the film business have praised and appreciated Hugh Grant's work. Their observations emphasize his charisma, adaptability, and important contributions to the film industry. This is an assemblage of opinions and insights from people who have collaborated with him and those who have evaluated his performances:

Filmmaker/writer Richard Curtis: Having collaborated with Grant on several classic movies, such as "Notting Hill," "Four Weddings and a Funeral," and "Love Actually," Curtis has frequently complimented Grant on his perfect comic timing and capacity to provide nuance to love characters. Grant is a "natural comedian" with a special talent for connecting with crowds, according to Curtis.

Emma Thompson, an actor: Grant's co-star in "Sense and Sensibility" and "Love Actually," Emma Thompson, has praised him for his humor and intellect. She has brought

Hugh Grant

attention to his ability to combine sensitivity with comedy in a way that makes his characters likable and accessible.

The director, Stephen Frears: - Director of "Florence Foster Jenkins" and "A Very English Scandal," Stephen Frears, has praised Grant's adaptability and readiness to take on difficult parts. According to Frears, Grant's performances are characterized by realism and nuance, which elevates the overall effect of his works.

Actress Renée Zellweger: - Grant's co-star in the "Bridget Jones" television series, Renée Zellweger, has lauded both his charm and expertise. She has stated that having Grant around the set added to the camaraderie and success of their work together by bringing a lighthearted and carefree vibe.

Film critic Roger Ebert: - The late Roger Ebert frequently complimented Grant's romantic comedy roles, highlighting his capacity to enhance the genre with his charm and wit. Ebert called Grant a "master of the romantic comedy" and emphasized how he could add interest and entertainment value to even the most formulaic of screenplays.

Based on Rolling Stone, Peter Travers: Grant's progress as an actor—moving from romantic comedies to more nuanced and somber roles—has been praised by Peter Travers. Grant's versatility and depth as an actor have been emphasized by Travers through his roles in movies such as "A Very English Scandal" and "Florence Foster Jenkins".

The Guardian: The Guardian's critics have frequently praised Grant's distinct charm and on-screen persona. Reviews have consistently noted his passion for portraying both endearing and problematic characters. His performance in "Paddington 2" was lauded by The Guardian as evidence of his continuing popularity and adaptability.

Variety: The critics at Variety have acknowledged Grant's impressive ventures into drama while also highlighting his constancy and dependability as a leading actor in romantic comedies. His performances are memorable and powerful because of his ability to strike a balance between comedy and passion, as reviews have frequently noted.

Major Ideas in Thoughts

Flexibility and Scope: - Grant's versatility has been widely noted by reviewers and colleagues alike, who have noted that he can play a variety of parts, from sophisticated serious roles to endearing love leads. One of the main reasons for his continuous success and critical praise has been his adaptability.

Charm & Screen Presence: Grant's innate charm and captivating on-screen persona are frequently cited as characteristics that set his performances apart. Those who have collaborated with him and evaluated his work have consistently noted his capacity to fascinate and engage audiences.

Hugh Grant

Dedication and Professionalism: - Many of his directors and co-stars have lauded Grant for his professionalism and commitment to his trade. His dedication to providing genuine and captivating performances has gained him recognition in the field.

Impact on Genre: A recurrent issue in Reflections is Grant's effect on the romantic comedy genre. His portrayals of romantic protagonists have redefined expectations and raised the bar, leaving a lasting impression on the genre.

Hugh Grant's career has been well-praised by reviewers and colleagues alike for his charisma, adaptability, and noteworthy contributions to the film industry. His standing as a gifted and significant actor has been cemented by his ability to strike a balance between comedy and emotional depth as well as his smooth transitions between genres. The opinions of individuals who have collaborated with him and evaluated his performances highlight his enduring influence on the motion picture business and popular culture.

Hugh Grant

Enduring Inputs into Film

Hugh Grant has left a lasting impression on the film business with his career, which is distinguished by outstanding performances. His work has had a variety of effects on popular culture and the film business. This is a comprehensive examination of his lasting influence and accomplishments:

1. Redefining the Romantic Comedy Genre: Hugh Grant's contribution to the revival of the romantic comedy genre in the 1990s and early 2000s is arguably his most well-known achievement. His performances, which combined charm, comedy, and sensitivity, gave the genre a new viewpoint.

- Iconic Roles: 1994's "Four Weddings and a Funeral":** Grant had a pivotal part in the genre as he portrayed Charles, a charming but imperfect romantic hero. The success of the movie proved that romantic comedies could be enjoyed by audiences and critics alike.

111

Hugh Grant

- "Notting Hill" (1999): Grant demonstrated his ability to blend romantic appeal with everyday relatability in his portrayal of William Thacker, a modest bookstore owner who falls in love with a well-known actress. The popularity of the movie contributed to Grant's reputation as the face of the contemporary romantic comedy.

- "Bridget Jones's Diary" (2001): Grant demonstrated his ability to combine romanticism with a hint of humorous villainy in his portrayal of the endearing but imperfect Daniel Cleaver. The movie's popularity aided in the revival of the genre and showed that romantic comedies could address sophisticated, modern subjects.

Impact: Grant's portrayal of a humorous yet deeply emotional romantic protagonist in these movies created a new template for the genre. His popularity affected romantic comedy performers and directors and opened the door for a new wave of romantic comedies.

2. Broadening the Purpose of British Film: Grant's work has been instrumental in bringing British film to a

worldwide audience. His popularity has increased awareness of British movies and creators abroad.

- Partnerships with British Talent: Working Title Films: Grant's partnerships with Working Title Films, which produced films such as "Love Actually," "Notting Hill," and "Four Weddings and a Funeral," were crucial to the prosperity of British cinema in the 1990s and early 2000s. His collaborations with filmmakers like as Stephen Frears and Richard Curtis helped introduce British storylines and talent to an international audience.

- Supporting British Talent: A lot of British actors saw their careers launched and sustained by Grant's films, which frequently included ensembles of these performers. His popularity has aided in raising awareness of British filmmaking and talent internationally.

Impact: British cinema became a powerful force in the film business thanks to Grant's global success. His work has promoted a wide variety of British tales and skills and helped bring British actors and directors to the attention of audiences throughout the world.

3. Showcasing Acting Versatility: Grant's ability to switch between tragic and romantic comedies has shown his flexibility as an actor and impacted how other performers approach genre variety.

- Diverse Roles: In "About a Boy" (2002), Grant demonstrated his ability to handle intricate, character-driven storytelling with his depiction of Will Freeman, a self-absorbed bachelor who eventually transforms into a compassionate person.

- "Florence Foster Jenkins" (2016): Grant showed his breadth and depth as an actor by balancing comedy and drama in his role as St. Clair Bayfield.

- "A Very English Scandal" (2018): Grant received praise from critics for his depiction of Jeremy Thorpe, a politician embroiled in a scandal, and the role demonstrated his ability to deal with complex and serious characters.

- Impact: Grant's seamless cross-genre performance has created a standard for actors to pursue a variety of roles and push themselves beyond stereotypes. His career serves as evidence that performers may forge successful careers by taking on a variety of roles and genres.

4. Promoting Press Reform and Media Ethics Conversations:

Because of Grant's activity, significant topics like press reform and media ethics are now being discussed in public.

- Leveson Inquiry and Hacked Off Campaign: Grant's evidence during the Leveson Inquiry was essential in analyzing media ethics and practices and advancing the conversation about the necessity of press accountability and regulation.

Hugh Grant

- Hacked Off Campaign: Grant has promoted a more moral press and more safeguards for people against mistreatment by the media by his participation in this campaign.

Impact: Grant's advocacy has impacted discussions about media ethics in the public sphere and helped initiatives to raise press standards. His campaign has brought attention to the issue of protecting people's right to privacy and ethical media.

5. Contributions to Film Production and Industry Advocacy: In addition to his acting career, Grant has made a significant contribution to the film industry through his work as a producer and industry champion.

- Film Production: - Producing Work: Through Simian Films, his firm, Grant has produced films. His producing work includes movies like "The Rewrite" (2014), in which he promoted indie filmmaking and helped to generate new ideas.

Hugh Grant

- business Advocacy: - Supporting Independent Films: Grant's participation in indie films and his encouragement of other film endeavors have enhanced the range of perspectives and narratives in the film business.

Impact: As a producer and industry champion, Grant's efforts have encouraged the growth of fresh ideas and a wide variety of viewpoints inside the motion picture business.

6. Cultural Influence via Enduring Characters: Hugh Grant's performances have given rise to enduring characters that captivate audiences and have a lasting impact on popular culture.

- Enduring Appeal - Memorable Performances: With phrases and sequences from movies like "Four Weddings and a Funeral" and "Notting Hill" still being well-known and regularly cited in popular culture, Grant's roles in these films have become cultural touchstones.

Hugh Grant

- Legacy: Grant's talent for developing endearing characters has made sure that his writing is still cherished and current by viewers. His status in cinematic history is cemented by the continued acclaim and revisitation of his pictures.

Hugh Grant's impact on film is evident in his ability to redefine the romantic comedy genre, broaden the audience for British films, showcase his flexibility as an actor, push for industry lobbying and film production, and advance conversations about media ethics. His enduring popularity and memorable roles have had a profound effect on popular culture and the film business. Throughout his career, Grant has shaped the direction of romantic comedies, elevated British actors to international prominence, and shown the importance of a flexible and committed performing career.

His efforts as a producer and advocate have helped the film business expand and diversify, and his advocacy has sparked crucial conversations about press reform and media ethics. Hugh Grant's filmography is full of

Hugh Grant

inspirational and entertaining moments, so his legacy will go on for a long time.

Hugh Grant

summary

Hugh Grant's transformation from a pleasant young actor to a well-respected personality in the public eye and the film business is evidence of his brilliance, adaptability, and timeless appeal. This book has examined his professional and personal life in detail, providing insights into how he has influenced film and other media for a long time.

From his early days as a talented actor in British theater and television to his debut as a leading man in romantic comedies, Grant's career has been marked by a remarkable transformation. His roles in movies like Notting Hill and Four Weddings and a Funeraldemonstrated his ability to combine humor with sincere feeling, raising the bar for the romantic comedy genre. His fame in these movies did more for him than just make him a household name; it brought a fresh take on the romantic hero, one who was endearing but yet flawed.

Hugh Grant

With the advancement of his career, Grant took on a greater variety of roles, showcasing his dramatic acting abilities in movies such as About a Boy and Florence Foster Jenkins. His career has been defined by his ability to go from lighthearted comedies to complicated, serious roles, demonstrating that he is not only a charming movie star but also a gifted actor who can take on a variety of difficult roles.

Grant's impact goes beyond his cinematic appearances. Both the film business and popular culture have greatly benefited from his efforts. His performances have made a lasting impression on both audiences and reviewers, and he has played a pivotal role in the development of the modern romantic comedy. His performances have produced enduringly beloved characters and situations that are still discussed and remembered.

Furthermore, Grant has made a significant contribution to British film. He has significantly contributed to raising the reputation of British cinema by collaborating with important British directors and promoting British

Hugh Grant

pictures abroad. His popularity has paved the way for a fresh batch of British actors and directors, bolstering the country's standing in the international cinema business.

Grant's activism work has been crucial in tackling significant societal concerns outside of his professional career. His involvement in the Leveson Inquiry and the Hacked Off movement raised awareness of the need for press accountability and media reform. Important discussions concerning the integrity of journalism and the defense of personal privacy have been spurred by his action.

Grant's dedication to changing the world is demonstrated by his support of several philanthropic initiatives, such as healthcare and refugee help. His charitable endeavors show that his influence transcends the big screen, impacting actual problems and helping people in need.

Hugh Grant's career serves as an example of the strength of ability combined with tenacity and creativity. His position as a prominent cultural figure has been

Hugh Grant

solidified by his ability to transition from romantic lead to serious performer in his acting career, as well as by his contributions to the film industry and social concerns.

Grant's contributions to film and society are still significant and relevant as long as people see his movies and appreciate his work. His career offers an illustration of how a prominent actor may utilize their position to bring about change and make a lasting impression.

The narrative of Hugh Grant is one of impact and metamorphosis. Through a combination of charm, cunning, and hard work, Grant has successfully navigated the difficulties of celebrity, from his early days as an aspiring actor to his current standing as a well-liked and respected figure in the film business. His contributions will be recognized for many years to come because of his accomplishments in the film industry and his social justice activities.

Hugh Grant's career and life have been examined in depth in this book, which has shown how his activism

Hugh Grant

and work have influenced not just his legacy but also the larger fields of film and society. Hugh Grant is undoubtedly a highly influential person in the entertainment industry and beyond when we consider his career. It is evident from looking back on it that his influence is broad and deep.

Hugh Grant is a vibrant and important public personality, as seen by his advocacy and career. He is a notable figure in both the arts and public life because of the way that his work has tackled significant societal concerns while simultaneously entertaining and inspiring audiences. His brilliance, integrity, and dedication to constructive change will surely live on in his legacy.

Hugh Grant

Printed in Great Britain
by Amazon